365 Dad Jokes

A Joke a Day That Your Dad Will Find Absolutely Hilarious. . . but Really Aren't!

Table Of Contents

Introduction

Hello!

Thanks for getting a copy of the *365 Dad Jokes: A Joke a Day That Your Dad Will Find Absolutely Hilarious . . . but Really Aren't!*

There are many hilarious *dad jokes* in this book—really bad jokes that will always make you laugh! This book is filled with puns that you can read to your friends and pass you off as a Wordsmith—except you *don't* have Smith as your last name.

There are jokes about work/school, family, relationships (wife/girlfriend, and others), the in-laws, health (aging and weight), children, and sports! When you get to read the chapter, you'll understand what I mean. It promises much but gives little.

I hope you enjoy every moment reading this book. But there's a disclaimer before you move on: reading this book in public *will* infect others with your boisterous and contagious laughter!

A lot of control has been put to exercise on the production of this book on dad jokes. I mean, think of the consequences. The other day, a mate of mine was at the doctor's. He got some not-so-good news. The doctor said, "You've only got ten to live."

My mate, in a total panic, asked urgently, "Ten what?" knowing he had his family, his finances, his car to pay off. "Weeks, months, years?"

"Nine . . ." said the doctor.

Mind you, in a panic over a thing completely blown out of proportion, we can end up at the surgery. I mean, bird flu—now we know it's perfectly tweetable, though it was going to turn into a pandemic.

When writing this book, we had your mental well-being in mind as well, not just your health. You can go insane reading some of these jokes. I mean, it's okay to end up in your own little world as long as you're known there. It's a known thing that really bad jokes make people indecisive. Maybe. And remember those little voices? At least they speak to you.

Read and tell yourself at the end of the day that you would be considered normal in some cultures. Being out of your mind is completely fine. It will help you come to terms with the jokes ahead. It's dark and scary there.

Chapter 1: Work

Work is a serious business. I mean, when I told everybody I wanted to be a joke writer, they used to laugh at me. I find nobody laughing now. But it's tough, isn't it? Work to me is like Christmas. You work your toes off, and the credit goes to the fat guy in the suit. In my coffee shop, I used to make the fresh cold drinks when I was much younger—you know, fresh lemonade, carbonated water, and crushed limes. But it was soda pressing, so I gave it up.

There's more to work than work, mind you. The social element is there as well. When I was strolling down the street the other day, there was a sign saying, "Help Wanted." I checked what was wrong. Then I was going to be an astronaut when I was older, but even before I started, I got fired.

My favorite hobby in the office is pressing F5—I find it so refreshing and entertaining. But not as entertaining as the below jokes.

1. Why is teamwork important?

It helps to put the blame on someone else.

2. Multitasking is something I'm good with.

I can procrastinate, be unproductive, and waste time all at once.

3. What ruins a Friday more than remembering that today is Tuesday?

Nothing!

4. I can't believe after taking just a day off, I got fired from the calendar factory.

5. My bad memory has actually caused me to lose my job.

I'm still employed but can't remember where.

6. Some people say the glass is half empty. Some say it's half full.

The engineers say the glass is twice as big as necessary.

7. I asked if the corporate wellness officer could teach me yoga.

He asked, "How flexible are you?"

"I can't make Tuesdays," I answered.

8. I always tell new hires, "Don't see me as your boss. See me as a friend who can get you fired."

9. What's in my résumé?

A list of things I hope you never ask me to do.

10. A man who buys his trainers off a drug dealer would end up tripping the whole day.

11. Construction worker's parties are the best.

They raise the roof.

12. The cheapest place to find a suit is from a deck of cards!

13. Do you want to know if a road worker is stealing at work?

Go to his house and look for the signs.

14. The best part of a 9–5 is the 5.

15. Start considering your retirement before your boss does.

That's the best time to do.

16. Do you want a secure job?

Go for one nobody else wants.

17. The cross-eyed teacher lost her job.

She couldn't control her pupils.

18. SON: I don't want to go to school. The teachers hate me, and I've got no friends.

MOTHER: Grow, son. You're the principal.

19. BOY: Sir, would you punish me for something I haven't done?

TEACHER: No, not at all.

BOY: Good, because I haven't done my homework.

20. You'd think a pirate's favorite letterrrrrr would be the *R* but it's actually the *C*.

21. A bear goes to a bar.

BEAR: Please, I'll have a . . . pint of beer.

BARTENDER: Why the big pause?

BEAR: Well, I've always had 'em!

22. For what reason did the can crusher leave his job?

It was soda pressing.

23. What is someone who doesn't like carbs called?

Lack-toast intolerant.

24. A man strolls into a bar, and it's empty, just the bartender and himself. He sits down and asks for a drink.

"Pssst . . . I like your tie," he heard someone whisper. The man glances around yet doesn't see anyone. "Pssst . . . that color is good on you."

He asks the bartender, "Hey, are you talking to me?"

Rolling his eyes, the bartender replies, "No, sorry about that. The peanuts are complimentary."

25. Why did the celebrant wrap himself in paper?

He desired to live in the present.

26. What is worn by a house?

A dress.

27. What did the empty glass hear the full glass say it?

You look drunk.

28. What form of transportation does a potato prefer?

The gravy train.

29. What did the ocean say to each other?

Nothing, they only waved.

30. Why should falling in love with a tennis player never be considered?

Love means *nothing* to them!

31. Why are pirates usually slow in learning the alphabet?

They spend years at *C*.

32. Why did the woman hang out with the mushroom?

He was a fun guy.

33. What does Snoop Dogg use an umbrella for?

Fo' drizzle.

34. What is common to politicians and diapers?

They need to be changed often because they both stink.

35. Why could the toilet paper not cross the road?

It got stuck in a crack.

36. Why did the bike choose not to go anywhere?

It was two-tired!

37. I said to my doctor, "I broke my arm in two places."

He replied, "Stop going to those places."

38. Christmas is just like your job, you do all the work, and all the credit goes to the fat guy in the suit.

39. How is an organization like a tree full of monkeys? All on different limbs at different levels. The monkeys on the bottom look up and see nothing but assholes while the monkeys on top look down and see a tree full of smiling faces.

40. A thief with a pistol stuck in a man's ribs said, "Let me have your money." Shocked by the sudden attack, the gentleman said, "I'm a congressman, you cannot do this!" The thief replied, "Then give me *my* money!"

41. When we're in a meeting, why do we "nod off to sleep"? It's so it looks like we're just agreeing with everything emphatically.

42. When an employment application asks, "In case of emergency, who should be notified? I always write, 'A competent doctor.'"

Chapter 2: School

It's only a school person that understands school humor and jokes the best. We've pulled together some favorite school-focused jokes so you can get some much-needed laughs.

We hope these bring you some medicine: laughter! These funny school puns and jokes are in a class of their own! They're, in fact, guaranteed to pass any hilarity test!

So whether you go short of words when it comes to language or geometry is your area, we hope our collection of the best school jokes brings you so much enjoyment.

43. Where's the fine line between the numerator and denominator.

It can only be seen by a fraction of guys.

44. What is an acid with an attitude called?

A-mean-oh acid.

45. What do you hate most about ancient history class?

The teacher tends to Babylon.

46. Why did the cold student sit at the corner?

He was told it was ninety degrees.

47. Do you know why sorority girls walk in odd numbers?

They can't even.

48. A tutor asked his students to make a sentence using the word *beans*.

STUDENT 1: My father grows beans.

STUDENT 2: My mother cooks beans.

STUDENT 3: We are all human beans.

49. At a Catholic school café, a nun places a note saying, "Only take one. God is watching," in front of a pile of apples. Further down the line is a heap of cookies. A little boy places his own note saying, "Take all you desire. God is watching the apples."

50. CHEMISTRY TEACHER: Oxygen was discovered in 1773. It is compulsory for breathing and life.

BLONDE STUDENT: Thank God I was given birth to after 1773. If not, I'd have died without it.

51. OLD TEACHER: Which tense is that if I say, "I am beautiful"?

Student: It is obviously past.

52. MATH TEACHER: If I have six bottles in my left hand and five in my right hand, what do I have?

STUDENT: A drinking problem.

53. TEACHER: What is the most important book in your life?

STUDENT: My dad's checkbook!

54. What happened when the antennas got married?

The ceremony was quite boring, but the reception was awesome.

55. Would you like to hear a pizza joke?

Yes, but please don't make it too cheesy!

56. Tell me why chemists are great at solving problems?

They have all the solutions!

57. What type of pants is worn by Mario and Luigi?

Denim, denim, denim.

58. I told my supervisor three organizations were after me and I would like a raise to remain at my job. We haggled for some minutes, and I settled for a 7 percent raise. On leaving his office, he stopped to ask, "By the way, which organizations are after you?" I replied, "The cable, gas, and electric company."

59. You can't be in the desert and starve . . . because of all the sand which is there!

60. Tell me why Chuck Norris cannot use the internet.

He won't submit.

61. Tell me what a nosy pepper does?

It gets jalapeño business.

62. Give me one reason we don't see elephants hiding in trees.

They're really good at it.

63. What did the left eye hear the right eye say?

Truthfully, something smells between you and me.

64. Why did John come fifth and get a toaster?

He was disobedient when God said to him, "Come forth and you shall get eternal life!"

65. I was gifted the world's worst thesaurus today.

It is not only terrible—it's terrible.

66. What did the doughnut go to a dentist for?

To get a filling.

67. How do you differentiate between a philosopher and a mathematician?

A philosopher can work without the trash bin, but the mathematician needs a pencil, paper, and a trash bin to work.

68. What lives in the ocean but is non-orientable?

Möbius Dick.

69. What made the giraffe get terrible grades?

His head was in the clouds.

70. How do you differentiate between a large pizza and a PhD in mathematics?

A large pizza can be used to feed a family of four.

71. What is the largest accumulation point of poles called?

Warsaw!

72. What is a music teacher with problems called?

A trebled man.

73. What killed the janitor?

He kicked the bucket.

74. What way can you determine the sex of a chromosome easily?

Pull its genes down.

75. What is the flooring in daycare centers called?

Infant-tile!

76. What is the result of crossing Curious George and Sonic the Hedgehog?

2 Fast 2 Curious.

77. What gets whiter as it gets dirtier?

Chalkboard.

78. Why did the music teacher ask for a ladder?

He needed to reach the high notes.

79. What is the leader of a biology gang called?

The nucleus.

80. What made the two 4s skip lunch?

They 8 (ate) earlier.

81. What bus would you never enter?

A syllabus.

82. What did the mathematician's parrot say to you?

A poly "no meal."

83. Why do chemistry teachers talk about ammonia a lot?

It's basic material.

84. We all know that H_2O is water, but what is H_2O_4?

Drinking, washing, bathing, swimming.

85. What did one math book tell the other?

Don't disturb me, I have enough problems.

86. What made the teacher write on the windows?

He wanted it to be very clear.

Chapter 3: Family

If it wasn't for my family, you wouldn't be reading this book now. Indeed, this chapter of jokes is dedicated to my brother. Yes, he saved my life when I was young. You see, I developed a dreadful disease when I was only a fledgling writer just learning to scribe my name. Eating a handful of dirt three times daily was the only way to survive. So, dear brother, thank you for pointing that out to me.

My family has been filled with both great people and tragedy. For example, my uncle was a great man, and we miss him much. He developed a condition as he got older—one that could only be treated by layering his back with spatulas of lard. We did our best, but we lost him fast.

I love my family. In fact, just the other day, I told my wife that every other weekend, I'd love to see my kids. She then reminded me that we were still married. A word of advice: be nice to your kids; it's always a wise thing to do. Not only do you love them, but someday, they'll be in the position to choose your nursing home.

In some weeks' time, my eldest will be flying back from university. My neighbor wanted to know if I was going to get him at the airport, but I replied that I'd known him since birth. My parents were loving and kind while I was growing up. There was me, Lana and Dana (my sisters), and my older brother Jim, who saved my life. Mom would never say who she loved most, bless her. However, she did reveal once that I was not in the top three.

Anyway, let's get on with a chapter on family dad jokes. Enough of prevarication (really, it's because my wife is saying if I don't get up and help her with the potatoes soon, she's going to ram my head into the computls fefdPksdf VegaBoJra boQdkg WorgjEfssor OGorgvvPGC-COREGO er.

87. An elderly couple is in the chapel. The wife whispers to her husband, "What should I do? I just let out a long, silent fart." The husband answers, "Most important of all is to replace your hearing aid's batteries!"

88. Wife: I saw you in my dream. You bought a diamond ring for me at a jewelry store.

Husband: I had a similar dream where your dad paid the bill.

89. MOTHER: Take a look at that kid at that corner. He isn't misbehaving.

SON: He probably has good parents then.

90. A mom sends, "Hi, son! What does IDK, ILY, & TTYL mean?" to her son, and he texts back, "I Don't Know, I Love You, and Talk To You Later." She replies, "It's fine. Don't worry yourself about it. I'll ask your brother. Love you too."

91. YOUNG BOY: Mom, I had a big fight with my classmate today. He called me a sissy.

MOTHER: What did you do?

YOUNG BOY: I hit him with my purse!

92. What's your most awkward family moment?

Getting a double-cheek kiss from you-know-who.

93. I put so much more effort into naming my first Wi-Fi than my first child.

94. If the beginning of women's holiday shopping season is Halloween, when is men's?

Christmas Eve.

95. When we go to the beach with the kids, we use a really strong sunblock. It's SPF 80. Squeeze the tube, a sweater comes out.

96. Why do you sometimes regret your first full-time job?

Because you were probably making more working as your parents' daughter while you were in college.

97. Hanging up with my ninety-two-year-old mom, I sighed, then told my ninety-eight-year-old uncle, "She's too stubborn." He shook his head thoughtfully and sympathetically and cautioned, "You'll experience difficulty with her as she gets older."

98. What's the only nice thing about naming your kid?

You don't have to add six numbers to ensure the name is available.

99. My kid ran to me, crying. "Mommy, I stubbed my toe," he said to me. I replied, "Let me kiss it and make it better. Which toe was it?" He replied, "The one with no roast beef."

100. My two-and-half-year-old sat with me in the bathroom, looking on as I removed my dentures and brushed them. She asked after a few minutes, "Do you take your ears off too?"

101. Where there's a will, there's a relative.

102. I asked my sister-in-law, the mother of four boys, "Would you still have kids if you were to do it all over again?"

"Yes," she said, "but not these four."

103. What is the best-ever backhanded compliment you've heard from a kid about a present?

"Thanks for the toys. I'll play with them when I'm bored."

104. My son saw a strange thing today.

He saw the zebra looking at a piano.

105. When I was a girl of thirteen, my mom was so ignorant, I could manage having the old woman around. When I became twenty-two, I was bewildered at how much the old woman had learned in nine years.

106. Why is Father's Day important?

Because, apart from being the day we honor dads, it's the only day of the year that any business is done by Brookstone.

107. I gave my dad $100 and told him, "Buy something that will make life easier for you." He went out and bought my mom a gift.

108. When I was younger, I had this disease that required I eat dirt twice a day in order to survive. I'm glad my elder brother informed me back then.

109. About two months before his death, my uncle covered his back in lard. Afterward, he went downhill fast.

110. I was cooking a surprise dinner for my family, but the fire truck's ruined it.

111. What is the hardest part of riding a scooter?

Informing your parents you're gay.

112. My father died when we couldn't remember his blood group. As he died, he continued admonishing us to "be positive," but it's difficult without him.

113. I'm writing a horror screenplay. It begins with a ringing phone. The person on the other ends is their mom saying, "I have a computer question."

114. One out of five individuals on earth is Chinese. My family is made up of five people, so one of them must be. It's either my dad or my mom. Or my younger brother Colin. Or my elder brother Ho-Cha-Chu. But something tells me it's Colin.

115. How did you know your road worker father was stealing from his job?

All the signs were there when I got home.

116. Why should I be pleasant to my children?

They'll select your nursing home.

117. BOY: Dad, have you had your hair cut?

DAD: No, I got them all done.

118. Why did the cookie cry?

His parents were a wafer so long.

119. What is a mountaineer's son called?

Cliff.

120. Why should good parents tell their children not to eat sushi?

It's a little fishy.

121. What do buffaloes say to their sons when they drop them off at school?

Bison.

122. What is a door-to-door salesman's son called?

Matt.

123. What did the little boy get when he told his mom to make him a sandwich?

She waved her magic wand.

124. What do gymnasts tell their parents when they fall in love?

She's head over heels.

125. What did the family of snowmen in a garden ask the rest?

"Hey, can you smell carrots?"

126. How do aliens organize their kid's birthday party?

They planet.

127. A mom took her son to buy some camouflage trousers.

But they couldn't find any.

128. What did the son say when his dad bought him a belt with a watch on it?

It was a "waist" of time.

129. How many months was Johnny jailed for when stole a calendar?

Twelve months.

130. At the end of a classic film *E.T.*, the dad asked his daughter what ET was short for?

She said, "'Cause he's only got tiny legs."

131. Why did the father tell his son to call him dad?

Because he promised to call him later.

132. What happened to the girl that tried to sell her batteries on eBay?

She gave them free of charge.

133. Why was pop spider and mom crossed with teenage spider?

He was spending too much time on the web.

134. Why did the girl's new bike fall over?

It was two-tired.

135. Why do your parents not want you to study technology?

They said it's artificial intelligence.

136. Where did Dad wake up after he slept like a log last night?

In the fireplace.

137. Dad and Mom went on a dinner date to celebrate their wedding anniversary. Dad requested for some condiments.

The waiter replied, "Your wife looks very beautiful."

138. Joey and Jimmy and Joey were playing out. While Joey messed about with a car battery, Jimmy found some old fireworks.

They were caught by the police. One was let off; the other was charged.

139. Why could Billy's mom not put down the book?

It was a book on the history of glue.

140. What did John call his pet fish with no eyes?

Fsh.

141. Why could nothing get under his skin?

Because he was a calm Daddy Skeleton.

142. Where do lazy people sell their books about all their achievements?

In the fantasy section.

143. What differentiates a scruffy son on his tricycle and a well-dressed dad on his bicycle?

Attire.

144. What made Mafia Mike buy his daughter a mink coat?

Fur protection.

145. What do you call a gardener's son?

Doug.

146. What does someone who isn't a gardener call his son?

Douglas.

Chapter 4: Relationships

My wife and I have an awesome relationship. My wife thinks marriage is very important. Our marriage is a bit like a brilliant free credit card. You know, each time we have something important to discuss, I start with enthusiasm. Halfway through, I get fed up and end up saying, "I agree." Speaking of credit cards, just the other day, mine got stolen. No, I didn't report it to the police; it was saving me money. My wife uses it more than the thief.

My wife and I have always had a superb relationship. At the birth of our first child, I was right there beside her. I remember it today and totally comprehend that she was stressed by the event. I shouted, "Push, push!" She replied, "You idiot stop shouting at me!" Well, it wasn't my fault the car broke down.

In all fairness, my wife is incredibly generous. I remember at her wedding, I was putting the gold band on her finger and feeling bad that she had four rings for me—two for my wrists and two for my ankles. Just so they wouldn't get lost, they even had little chains between them.

This touching little tale is going to be the last one. Just the other day, my wife came up to me. She looked really excited. Beaming from ear to ear, carrying some clothing, she cried, "Look, darling, this cloth was bought thirty years ago, and it's still well fitting." And I have to say it was a beautiful scarf.

Enough of the waiting. Here's a chapter full of jokes about marriage and relationships.

147. Do you have a Valentine's Day date?

Yes, it's February 14.

148. Why shouldn't you break up with a goalie?

He is a keeper.

149. What did the two boats hear the third boat ask?

Who's interested in a little row-mance?

150. What did the patient whose leg broke in an accident say to her doctor?

I have a crutch on you, my doc.

151. Why did your doctor call me a parasite?

You are in my mind, my heart, and in my entire body.

152. I met my girlfriend on the internet. My dad asked what line I used on her.

I replied, "Just a modem."

153. A couple is on a dinner date at an exotic restaurant. The woman tells her man to say something that'll make her heart race. "I forgot my wallet," he replied.

154. Why do you think painters will fall for their models?

They love their models with all their art.

155. What is the perfect crime a couple can commit together?

Stealing each other's heart.

156. Why is the brain the most impressive organ in the whole of our body?

It works 24/7 from the day we are born right up until you fall in love.

157. Why is love a form of amnesia?

A boy forgets that there are about 3.2 billion other girls in the world.

158. A *T. rex* told her boyfriend, "I love you this much," as she stretched out her arms. To which the boyfriend replied, "That's not very much at all!"

159. What would you rather choose, men or shoes?

Shoes. They last longer.

160. GIRLFRIEND: How would you describe me?

BOYFRIEND: *ABCDEFGHIJK.*

GIRLFRIEND: What does that mean?

BOYFRIEND: Amazing, beautiful, cute, dutiful, elegant,

fabulous, gorgeous, and hot.

GIRLFRIEND: Awww, thank you. So what about IJK?

BOYFRIEND: I'm just kidding!

161. Disregard the butterflies. Every time I'm with you, I feel the entire zoo.

162. What is the best definition of love?

Not having to hold in your gas anymore.

163. Why do you need a bandage?

Because I just scraped my knee falling for you.

164. Why is love a lot like peeing in your pants?

The warm sensation can be felt only by you.

165. What did one volcano say to the other?

I lava you.

166. How do you differentiate between herpes and love?

Love does not last forever.

167. Can I crash at your place tonight?

Is your name Microsoft?

168. My love for everyone is real.

I love to be around some people, I love to avoid some people, and I would love to punch some people in the face.

169. You are like asthma to me.

You just take my breath away.

170. You are like dandruff to me.

No matter how hard I try, I just cannot get you out of my head.

171. You are like my dentures.

Without you, I cannot smile.

172. You are just like my car.

You drive me crazy.

173. Why are men fond of falling in love at first sight?

It saves them a lot of money.

174. What is the funniest joke of all time?

My love life.

175. Explain falling in love in your own words.

It's like going deep into a river. Getting out of it is much more difficult than it is to get in.

176. Can you borrow me a kiss?

I promise to return it.

177. Never laugh at your partner's choices.

You are one of them.

178. Why do you call your partner Wi-Fi?

I feel such a strong connection around her.

179. Two antennas met on a roof, fell in love, and decided to get married.

They had a terrible ceremony, but the connection looks so strong.

180. What is love?

Love is . . . getting mad at a person, telling the person to go to hell, and wishing they have a safe trip there.

181. What is that tingly feeling that runs through your body when feelings for someone begin to well up inside you?

That's you losing your common sense.

182. If you don't fall from the sky or a tree, what other way can a girl fall?

Fall in love with me.

183. Why do you think we are both subatomic particles?

I feel a strong force between the both of us.

184. I wish I could rearrange the alphabet.

U and *I* would be together.

185. What happens every time two vampires meet and decide to hang out?

Love at first bite!

186. I would like us to go fishing together.

I really want us to hook up.

187. Is Google female or male?

Definitely female. It doesn't let you end your sentence before suggesting an idea.

188. TEACHER: If your father earns $400 per week and gives your mother half of it, what will he have?

JOHNNY: A heart attack.

189. WIFE: I had a good sleep where I just had a dream that you gifted me a diamond necklace. Could you tell me what this means?

HUSBAND: You'll know tonight.

The man came home that evening with a small package and gifted it to his wife. Glad she unboxed it and found a book titled *The Meaning of Dreams*.

Chapter 5: The In-Laws

Although marriage now in almost every part of the world is based on personal preference and common interests, in today's humor, we have remnants of the past. Jokes portray the ambivalence between generations.

Fathers-in-law are portrayed as ridiculously bereft at the loss of their daughters. Mothers-in-law are depicted as meddlesome. There's just a little love between mothers and daughters-in-law. Sons-in-law are displayed as lovable oafs, though inadequate. In some jokes, one's perspectives determine one's feelings about their in-laws. Jokes from the adult children's perspective show their ambivalence. The in-law children, like their parents, find it difficult to cope with differences in lifestyle, differences in belief and expectations. Some of these jokes are just very wicked.

Someone was going to work recently, and he sees a crowd of people walking. Looking ahead, he sees a gentleman in front of a coffin with a little dog, followed by the crowd.

He met the owner, and he asked him, "Man, what happened here?"

He replied, "Pff, my mother-in-law died."

"Eh, how sad . . . And if I may ask, how?"

"She was bitten by my dog . . ."

"You don't tell me! Could you please lend him to me for just tonight?"

"Get in line!"

Because these jokes encapsulate grains of truth, they live on.

190. What is the punishment for bigamy?

Two mothers-in-law.

191. EMPLOYEE: Sir, I desire to have a day off to visit my mother-in-law next week.

BOSS: You can't have it.

EMPLOYEE: Thanks so much, sir! I always trusted you to be understanding.

192. So Johnny is finally engaged and so excited to show off his fiancée.

JOHNNY: Ma, I'm going to bring home five girls, and I would like you to guess my fiancée among them.

(Johnny walks in the door twenty minutes later with five girls behind him.)

MOM: That's her!

JOHNNY: Holy cow, how on earth did you know it was her?

MOM: I just don't like her.

193. At a magic show, after one specifically fantastic trick:

JOHNNY: Wow, how did you do that?

MAGICIAN: I would tell you, but then I'd have to kill you.

JOHNNY: Can you tell my mother-in-law?

194. A man was driving with his wife beside him and his mother-in-law in the back seat.

They won't just leave him alone.

MOTHER-IN-LAW: You're driving too fast!

WIFE: Stay more to the left.

After about twelve mixed orders, the man faces his wife

and asks, "Are you the one driving this car or your mother?"

195. SON: How do you differentiate between an accident and a tragedy?

FATHER: An accident is when you suddenly push your mother-in-law into a pool while a tragedy is if she swims and gets out.

196. CANNIBAL 1: I just can't stand my mother-in-law.

CANNIBAL 2: That's quite understandable. However, I'll suggest you have the potatoes with the gravy?

197. FRIEND 1: My mother-in-law is an angel.

FRIEND 2: You're a lucky man. Mine is still alive.

198. Why would you rather manage a vicious dog rather than your father-in-law?

A vicious dog eventually let us go!

199. Why do you want to be buried next to the Krispy Kreme when you die?

At least my daughter-in-law gets to visit me there.

200. What does a golfer call a hit ball that misses the green by inches?

A son-in-law shot. It's not your expectations, but you'll take it.

201. OLD MAN 1: My daughter married an amazing man. He cleans, cooks, and gets the kids off to school.

OLD MAN 2: My son married a lazy woman. She makes him clean, cook, and get the kids off to school.

202. How would you define *mixed feelings*?

When your Maserati goes over a cliff, but your mother-in-law was in it.

203. CUSTOMER: What legal information do I need to buy arsenic?

PHARMACIST: Definitely not just this picture of your

mother-in-law.

204. Why was your mother-in-law banned from playing poker internationally?

She keeps all the chips on her shoulder.

205. Why were Adam and Eve the luckiest and happiest couple in the world?

Neither of them had a mother-in-law.

206. How do you differentiate between in-laws and outlaws?

Outlaws are wanted.

207. What happened when you took your mother-in-law to the Madame Tussaud's chamber of horrors?

"Keep her moving, sir. We're stocktaking," said one of the attendants.

208. Mother-in-law canceled her tomorrow's funeral.

DAVID: I was sorry to hear about your mother-in-law's death. What was the complaint?

JOHNNY: We haven't had any yet.

209. My doorbell rang this afternoon. When I opened the door, I saw my mother-in-law standing on the front step.

"Can I stay here for a few days?" she said.

"Sure you can," I replied and shut the door in her face.

210. What happened at your mother-in-law's funeral?

They pulled her up and down three times till people had stopped applauding!

211. My mom said she'll die if I marry you.

Just the perfect wedding gift for me.

212. Thank you for coming by, Grandma.

This morning, Dad said that the only missing thing was

you visiting.

213. What do men consider the most dangerous thing their mother-in-law ever did?

Giving birth to their wife.

214. What slowly falls toward the earth yet doesn't stop the fall till it reaches hell?

Your mother-in-law who ran away from paradise!

215. Did the defendant hit his mother-in-law?

Yes, Your Honor!

And you didn't intervene?

It was as if he could deal with her himself!

216. The feeble mother-in-law is the best mother-in-law for her.

When she arrives in a taxi, you simply exit and say, "Thank you for visiting. Have a nice journey back home!"

217. A man attempted to drown his sorrow; however, it didn't work.

His mother-in-law could swim!

218. How do you differentiate between a vulture and a mother-in-law?

Vultures only assault when you are dead.

219. In court:

Were they convicted recently?

The previous summer, my mother-in-law was with us for two months!

220. I get sick every Christmas, and it lasts for around seven days. And then my mother-in-law goes back.

221. "I realize that you desire for me to die," the mother-in-law stated, "so you will probably dance and jump on my grave."

"That won't happen, you know how much I despise standing in lines."

222. LITTLE BOY: Dad, what is Adam's mother-in-law called?

FATHER: He didn't have one. Have you forgotten he was living in a paradise?

223. I have just had a really beautiful trip.

I dropped off my husband's mom at the airport.

224. DAVID: Their mother-in-law just fell into the lion's den.

JANE: What are they doing about it?

DAVID: No, she has to find her own way out.

JANE: I'd like to pay for the lion's den when she comes out.

225. "It was me who saved my mother-in-law from drowning."

"Hmmmmm, okay, do you have other confessions?"

226. When her husband came back from work, the newlywed wife announced to him, "I have great news for you. Very soon, we would be three in this house rather than two."

With a smile on her face, her husband ran to her. His clearly had delight in his eyes.

With all the glow of happiness in him, he was kissing his wife passionately when she said, "I'm happy you feel this way. From tomorrow morning, my mother will move in with us."

Chapter 6: Health

The truth is, there is a close link between life and food. I mean, you're the best thing since sliced bread this day, then you're toast the next. So we'll begin this chapter with a health warning. We know that smoking kills, obesity kills! Too much bacon kills! But smoking bacon cures it.

So most of us, in order to lose some additional pounds, have tried to diet at least once. I began my new diet by doing away with all the fattening food in my kitchen. It was delicious.

I was almost turning into a vegan but knew that was going to be a big missed steak.

My wife just turned a vegan. That's what I thought, although she was who she was before.

I just burned 2,000 calories. That's a good news. Must remember to bring the brownies out of the oven early enough.

When changing our diet or dieting, sometimes we can feel like we are in a barren desert that is dry. We've changed what we ate, how much we ate, and when we ate; and we've even given up our favorite foods. Also, most of us realized that dieting is not an easy task at all even though it's necessary for our well-being. I have made a collection of a few jokes on weight loss just so this desert looks a little bit more succulent. Why not try them? If you want a way to cope with.

227. For what reason did the diet coach send her customers to the paint store?

She was told you could get slimmer there.

228. I'm not intrigued by any diet plan.

Except it allows me to use rollover calories.

229. My observation when I'm on a diet is that instead of saying, "I ate nachos," I would say, "I accidentally ate nachos."

230. What do you call somebody who can't stick with a diet routine?

A desserter.

231. I had a salad for dinner! Basically, tomatoes and croutons. I mean, one big round crouton garnished with tomato sauce. Oh, and cheese. Okay, fine, it was a pizza. I had a pizza.

232. What is a non-amateur live bacterium called?

A probiotic.

233. I choked on a carrot this evening, and all I could imagine was "A doughnut wouldn't dare do this to me."

234. I detest brushing my teeth in the night because it connotes I can't have any more nourishment for my body.

I'm simply never prepared for that level of commitment.

235. After exercising once, I found out I was allergic to it. My heart raced, my skin flushed, I got sweaty, and became short of breath.

It is very dangerous.

236. Why can't ladies drop five pounds?

Because they won't let go of their purse.

237. All my life, I thought air was free.

But then I bought a bag of chips.

238. What is an American celebrity who starts a weight-loss trend called?

Johnny Applecidervinegar.

239. Someone told me I gained weight.

I replied, "I'm in a westward expansion process."

240. What superfood does the terracotta figurine love most?

Ch-ch-ch-chia seeds.

241. I don't need a fitness coach trainer as much as I need somebody to chase me around and slap those unhealthy foods off my hand.

242. "Wow, I was really filled up by that lean cuisine" was never said by anyone.

243. What was the Holy Roman Empire's most popular weight-loss trend?

The diet of worms.

245. What does the Energizer bunny use to stay in shape?

The alkaline diet.

246. Today I purchased a cupcake but without the sprinkles.

Diets are difficult.

247. NUTRITIONIST: You should eat 1,200 calories per day.

ME: That's cool, and how many per night?

248. I strongly desire to work out, but then I strongly desire to not work out even more.

249. I never saw myself as the type of person who would wake up so early in the morning to an exercise routine.

One of the few correct pastime predictions of myself.

250. I have to begin eating healthier foods, but first I have to eat all the junks in the house so that I'm not tempted by it anymore.

251. The house is loaded with the stuff because my wife is on a tropical food diet.

It's enough to make a mango insane.

252. I'm on a seafood diet.

I eat when I see food.

253. I only appear to recollect I have to shed some pounds after eating nine cookies.

254. What exercise do you love the most?

Chewing.

255. Every time I try to lose weight, it finds me.

256. It took a great deal of willpower and self-discipline.

But I finally stopped dieting.

257. For what health reasons did you stop jogging?

My thighs continued rubbing together, setting my pantyhose ablaze every time.

258. Remember, you are what you eat.

I need to eat somebody skinny.

259. If the plan was for us not to have midnight snacks, why does the fridge have a light?

260. The garlic diet: You don't shed weight; you only look thinner from a distance.

261. Welcome to the weight-loss platform.

Double-click the mouse ten million times to lose one pound.

262. Why can't mosquitoes suck fat instead of blood?

263. Define calories.

They are tiny creatures that live in your wardrobe and sew your outfits a little tighter every night.

264. There's an odd new trend at my workplace. Employees naming the foods in the company fridge. Today I ate Kevin, a tuna sandwich.

265. "Your request please."

"The XXL fries, nine chicken strips, and three hamburgers."

"Add a Diet Coke."

266. A lot of people add weight by having cozy dinners for two . . . alone.

267. My fitness trainer instructed me to bend down and touch my toes. "That's a kind of relationship I don't have with my feet. Can I just wave?" I replied.

Chapter 7: Children

"Knock, knock!"

"Who's there?"

"It's Our."

"Our what?"

"Our funny jokes."

I remember one of the holidays my kids had with their friends around. The heavy rain started just when they were about to go out to play. Just when they were almost going to start cursing and swearing in the rain, one more friend of my kids in the rain came knocking. He wanted to join in playing with the other bored children. "Who's that?" I asked, and there it was. The jokes for kids started.

These jokes beat the boredom out of them and kept them engrossed together for hours. And oh, just when it seems to me like they are not educative, I realized it got them thinking and alert in giving answers that are swift—of course, all had pun. Not long, they got a hand of it and came up with their own jokes. It looked like throughout the holidays, that was all they did.

Now did your brain get you thinking at the sound of my

knock? Oh yeah, there you have the idea. I remember in the earlier paragraph I said it's probably not educative. Well, take it however you want, that's it.

If you think kids are too young to understand jokes, then you may want to have a rethink. Kids are actually punsters. Below is the list of some of the collected kid-friendly jokes that were told that holiday period.

268. FATHER: What is a sleeping dinosaur called?

SON: A dino-snore!

269. FATHER: What is a rocket?

SON: A fast, loud, and crunchy chip!

270. MOTHER: What made the teddy bear say no to dessert?

DAUGHTER: Because she was stuffed.

271. FATHER: What has ears but cannot hear?

DAUGHTER: A cornfield.

272. TEACHER: What is the result of crossing a snowman and a vampire?

DANIEL: Frostbite!

273. MOTHER: What did one plate say to the other plate?

JOHNNY: Dinner is on me!

274. JOHNNY: What made the student eat his homework?

JANE: Because the teacher told him it was a piece of cake!

275. JOHNNY: When you search for something that's lost, why do you always find it in the last place you searched?

JANE: Because you stop searching when you find it.

276. JANE: What is brown, hairy, and wears sunglasses?

MOM: A coconut on vacation.

277. FATHER: What did one pickle say to the other when they fell onto the floor?

SON: Dill with it.

278. TEACHER: What did the Dalmatian say after lunch?

JANE: That hit the spot!

279. PRINCIPAL: Why did the kid cross the playground?

TEACHER: To get to the other slide.

280. KID: How does a vampire start a letter?

ELDER BROTHER: Tomb it may concern . . .

281. KID: What do you call a droid that takes the long way around?

DEVELOPER: Android.

282. DAUGHTER: How do you stop an astronaut's child from crying?

MOM: You rocket!

283. TEACHER: Why was 6 afraid of 7?

JOHNNY: Because 7, 8, 9.

284. TEACHER: What subject do witches love most?

JANE: Spelling!

285. SON: What makes a joke become a dad joke?

FATHER: When the punchline is a parent.

286. DAUGHTER: How is a lemon drop made?

MOM: Just let it fall.

287. BOY: What would you do if you broke your arm in two places?

LITTLE BROTHER: I surely wouldn't go back to those two places.

288. JAY: What is your brother's position in the school football team?

MAY: He's one of the drawbacks, I guess.

289. BIG BROTHER: The planet over there is Mars.

LITTLE BROTHER: Then the one over there must be Pa's.

290. MOTHER: I hear you skipped school to play football.

SON: I didn't, Mom, and I have a fish to prove it.

291. MOTHER: Wow, your hair is growing so fast! You need a haircut again.

LITTLE JOHNNY: Maybe you should stop watering it so much whenever you're bathing me.

292. MOTHER: Why don't you ever want to have kids?

LITTLE GIRl: I hear they take nine months to download.

293. JOE'S MOTHER: It's such a nice day. I'd like to take Joe to the zoo.

JOE'S FATHER: Don't bother. Let them come and get him if they want him.

294. JANE: Why does Santa Claus not have any children?

Mother: Because he comes down the chimney only once a year.

295. MOTHER: I'm sure you enjoyed your first day at school. What did you learn today?

KID: Not enough. I should go back tomorrow.

296. If a thirty-five-year-old woman thinks of having children, what does a thirty-five-year-old man think of?

Dating them.

297. MOTHER: Why did you say computer games don't influence children?

TEENAGER: If Pacman would have influenced us as kids, we would now be running around in darkened rooms, munching on pills and listening to music on repeat mode.

298. TEACHER: Why do traffic lights turn red?

JOHNNY: You would as well, only if you had to stop and go in the middle of the road.

299. TEACHER: What happens when you take the school bus home?

JANE: The police make you bring it back.

300. BOY: My little sister is only in nursery school, and she's so smart! She can spell her name forward and backward.

GIRL: Wow, what's her name?

BOY: Hannah.

301. MOTHER: What exactly are you first at in school?

JUNIOR: Well, Mom, I'm first out when the bell rings!

302. JANE: Did you hear about the little girl who used a mirror to copy her friend's arithmetic test paper?

JOHN: She got all her answers backward. She got a grade of 39, and her friend got a grade of 93.

303. BOY 1: Where do blue eggs come from?

BOY 2: From sad chickens.

304. MISS JOHNSON: George, what kind of bird do you like best?

GEORGE: Fried chicken.

305. TUTOR: In this box, I have a ten-foot snake.

JOHN: You can't fool me, sir. Snakes don't have feet.

306. Two kids were talking to with other. One said, "I'm very worried. My dad works for twelve hours per day just to give me good food and a nice home. My mom cleans and cooks for me for the whole day. I'm worried sick!"

The other kid asks, "Why do you worry? To me, I think

you've made it!"

The first kid replies, "What if they try to escape?"

307. TEACHER: Order, children! Order!

JOHN: I'll have a burger with French fries.

308. MAY: Can a chicken be said to be good enough to eat when it's two weeks old?

MOTHER: No, dear.

MAY: How then does it manage to live?

309. TEACHER: It's clear that you haven't been studying your geography. What reason would you give?

JOHNNY: Well, my dad says the world changes every day. I'm choosing to wait a while till it settles down.

310. Kenny's teacher rewards his students' good work by putting a gold star on top of their homework. One day Kenny came home with a huge zero on his homework.

MOTHER: Kenny, what does this mean?

KENNY: Oh, my teacher ran out of stars. He gave me a moon.

311. TEACHER: Define an island.

MAY: It is a mass of land surrounded by water except in a place.

TEACHER: What place is it?

MAY: The top.

312. TEACHER: If one and one equals two, and two and two equals four, what does four and four make?

JOHNNY: That's not fair. You leave the hard ones for us and answer the easy ones yourself.

313. JANE: Why has our teacher asked us for three days how two and two is?

JOHNNY: She has a bad memory.

314. TEACHER: Abraham Lincoln had a hard childhood. He had to walk about nine miles to school every day.

NORMAN: It was his own fault. Why couldn't he wake up early to catch the school bus like everyone else?

315. TEACHER: Johnny, why don't you answer me?

JOHNNY: I did, Teacher. I shook my head.

TEACHER: How do you expect me to hear it rattle from down here?

Chapter 8: Sports

The present-day athletes are super serious. It's like they've got a way to home-run the humor from their bodies with their actions, results, strict workout regimen, and diet. I think it's time that they were taken down one or two pegs. This is the reason this list of funny jokes has been put together about athletes and the sports that they love. Whether it's soccer, football, or basketball (or any other sport that's okay), on this list there's a quick one-liner or a pun to bring out the laughter in even the most strident of sports fans.

Chicken soccer players, super tall basketball guys, leper hockey players, we have them all covered on this list. And here, there aren't any creepy Kobe jokes, don't worry. We've got some really funny humor collected on this list for the whole family. We've got nothing for your family if they're a bunch of sports-hating nerds. On this list, whatever your favorite sport is, we have a joke that's guaranteed to turn your baseball brain into a bullpen of laughter. Or they'll probably make the little Marv Albert in your brain say, "BOOMSHAKALAKA!" with joy. If there's no joke about your favorite sports game on this list, too bad.

Imagine, after some football fans in Nebraska were treated to a particularly painful loss earlier in the season, a woman called a sports-radio talk-show host and said, "Everybody should phone in and give at least one word for the game."

"What is your word?" the host answered.

"Bored out of my mind," answered the caller.

But on a serious note, we blew out the doors on these sports jokes, we even have a joke on this list about cricket.

316. Q: What kinds of stories do basketball players tell?

A: Tall tales!

317. Q: Why did the dog choose not to play football?

A: It was a boxer.

318. Q: How did the basketball get wet?

A: The players dribbled all over it.

319. Q: Why don't grasshoppers go to many football matches?

A: They prefer cricket matches!

320. Q: What made Cinderella get kicked off the baseball team?

A: She ran away from the ball!

321. Q: What is served but never eaten?

A: A volleyball!

322. Q: How do baseball players cool off?

A: They sit next to their fans!

323. Q: Where do old bowling balls land?

A: In the gutter!

324. Q: What's a subject does a runner love most?

A: Jog-raphy!

325. Q: What made Cinderella such a lousy baseball player?

A: Her coach was a pumpkin.

326. Q: What's the most depressing thing about tennis?

A: No matter how good you get, you can never be as good as a wall.

327. Q: How many NCAA players would it take to change a light bulb?

A: One. But he gets a car, money, and three hours of credit for it.

328. Q: Why made the referees stop the leper hockey game?

A: There was a face-off in the corner.

329. Q: What is common to a hockey player and a magician?

A: They both do hat tricks.

330. Q: What kind of tea do hockey players drink?

A: Penaltea!

331. Q: Why was the chicken sent off?

A: For persistent fowl play!

332. Q: What insect played badly at quarterback?

A: The fumble-bee!

333. Q: What makes managers come along to away games with briefcases?

A: So they can pack the defense!

334. Q: What is similar to a volleyball player and a carpenter?

A: They both hammer spikes!

335. Q: How many golfers would it take to change a light bulb?

A: Fore!

336. Q: What can a soccer team do when the pitch is flooded?

A: Bring on their subs!

337. Q: Do you know how hens encourage their baseball teams?

A: They egg them on!

338. Q: Do you know where religious children do sports?

A: On the prayground!

339. Q: What's a tennis player's favorite city?

A: Volleywood!

340. Q: How does a physicist exorcize?

A: By pumping ion!

341. Q: What happened to the one about the bad pole vaulter?

A: It never goes over very well.

342. Q: What happened when the boating store had a big sale on canoes?

A: It was quite the oar deal.

343. Q. Why should you not consider marrying a tennis player?

A. Love means nothing to them.

344. Q. Why did the golfer wear two pairs of pants?

A. In case he got a hole in one.

345. Q: Why don't women play football?

A: Eleven of them would not wear the same outfit in public.

346. Q: What is the problem with jogging?

A: It'll be too far to walk back by the time you realize you're not in shape for it.

347. Q: What is Michael Phelps in Chinese?

A: Ka Ching.

348. Q: What did the coach tell the broken vending machine?

A: Give me my quarter back!

349. Q: What made the basketballer come along to the game with his suitcase?

A: He traveled a lot!

340. Q: What is the similarity between a baseball player and a spider?

A: He catches a fly!

351. Q: What is the similarity between a baseball team and a pancake?

A: They both need a good batter!

352. Q: What sport does an insect love most?

A: Cricket!

353. Q: What is harder to catch when you run faster?

A: Your breath!

354. Q: What made basketball players love doughnuts?

A: They can dunk them!

355. Q: What did the ball hear a baseball glove say?

A: Catch you later!

356. Q: What animal hit a baseball best?

A: A bat!

357. Q: What eighteen-legged thing catches flies?

A: A baseball team!

358. Q: What never moves yet goes around a baseball field?

A: The fence!

359. Q: Why are all pro athletes bilingual?

A: They speak profanity and English.

361. Q: What is the one thing you've learned from the World Cup?

A: Europe still hasn't mastered the haircut.

360. Why doesn't it disturb anybody that "the Los Angeles Angels" baseball team directly translates to "the the angels angels"?

361. I get inside fast if lightning starts and I'm on the course. Let God if he wants to play through.

362. Swimming is a sport of confusion because sometimes you do to not die and other times you do it for fun.

363. Halfway through dinner one night, my friend John told me of his days as a defensive lineman playing football in college. His wife then asked me, "Jim, did you do sports in college?" I answered, "Yes, I was on a shooting team of West Point." Apparently impressed, she said, "That's great. Offense or defense?"

364. I have a higher preference for the tight yoga pants worn by football players over the frumpy businesswoman slacks worn by baseball players.

365. Does anyone think women talk too much? Try to sit through a six-hour pregame show of Super Bowl.

366. Leap-year joke:

Q: What do athletes wear on leap day?

A: Jumpsuits.

Conclusion

Hello again!

Thanks again for purchasing *A Joke a Day That Your Dad Will Find Absolutely Hilarious...but Really Aren't!*

I hope you loved and are recovering from these hilarious jokes! If you enjoyed the book, please do tell your friends about this book in case they could use a laugh.

And going by their looks, I'm sure they do!

So let's end with some lifestyle thoughts just for you— like a blunt knife, they didn't quite make the final cut.

Some advice on technology: Delete all your German contacts if you want a hands-free phone.

Everyone knows that Kim Kardashian's huge ass is a burden to her . . . but we've got not enough time here to discuss Kanye West.

Take this relieving thought away with you that no matter how hard a breakup with a partner can be, every time clowns divorce, it leads to a custardy battle.

So unless it is about being naked in the classroom, live

your dreams.

When you take up bonsai, it means bigotry is not your thing.

Make a stand against terrorism—wear a dress if you are a woman. And if you are a man, wear a dress still.

Look on the bright side always. If your kids are costing you a fortune, at least thank goodness the Spice Girls are no more. My daughter's favorite was Posh, and saffron is dead expensive.

Another good piece of news—you probably didn't grow up in Arkansas. If you've never been to Arkansas, imagine Walmart opened a country.

Speaking of countries, if you've never been to Dubai, just imagine you gave your eleven-year-old a trillion bucks to decorate their bedroom.

Anyway, got to go and tend to my cat. It's just recovering from a massive stroke.

Well, and just to prove I'm not some sort of schizophrenic idiot, this is goodbye from all of me, myself, and I.

Made in the USA
Lexington, KY
06 November 2019

56683710R00058